AF530249

Whole in Love

Healing, Loving, and Being Real in Relationships

Dr. Ifshan Mehraj

Qurate
quratebooks.com

Whole in Love: Healing, Loving, and Being Real in Relationships
Dr. Ifshan Mehraj

© Dr. Ifshan Mehraj

Published in 2025

© Published by

Qurate
quratebooks.com

Qurate Books Pvt. Ltd.
Goa 403523, India
www.quratebooks.com
Tel: 1800-210-6527, Email: info@quratebooks.com

All rights reserved
No part of this publication may be reproduced, stored in a retrieval system, or transmitted in any form or by any means, electronic, mechanical, photocopying, recording or otherwise, without the prior permission of the author.

ISBN: 978-93-58985-22-1

Contents

Part 1: My Story

ONE

Where It All Began

They say the way we love begins in childhood. And for me, love was something I had to earn. I was a child who observed more than she spoke – quiet, perceptive, and always attuned to the emotions in the room. I learned early that being good meant being accepted. That approval had to be maintained. That love came with expectations.

My parents did love me – but their love often felt conditional, shaped by cultural expectations and silent comparisons. I was appreciated, yes, but usually after I had done something to prove myself. I began to associate love with effort, acceptance with performance. I didn't know then that this would become the pattern I'd carry into every relationship.

The urge to be perfect seeped into my bones. I studied hard, stayed polite, tried not to make noise. I didn't know how to express hurt or ask for comfort. I didn't know that love could be safe without being earned. I just kept trying to be enough.

Over time, I became someone who gave and gave – even when my own needs weren't met. Especially then. Giving became my way of feeling needed. And needing? That felt like weakness.

But what I didn't realise was that this form of love – so full of self-sacrifice and silence – was slowly emptying me.

This chapter isn't about blame. It's about understanding. About naming the origin of the ache. Because healing only begins when we know where the wound lives.

And mine began here – in a quiet home, in the soft ache of always trying to be good enough.

Looking back, I see how I became a girl who apologised before speaking, who waited for praise to feel visible. I was scared of being misunderstood, scared of being too loud, too emotional, too much. I lived with the weight of invisible expectations – to be strong but gentle, quiet but perfect, giving but never asking.

I never quite knew what I needed, because I never had the space to explore those needs without judgment. I buried desires deep, convincing myself that being low-maintenance made me worthy. I didn't know then that true worthiness never needs to be earned – only remembered.

And so this chapter also becomes a gentle invitation – for you, the reader – to look at where your stories began. What did love look like for you as a child? What did you learn to suppress just to feel safe?

Because that's where the thread begins.

And until we trace that thread, we keep tying ourselves to people and patterns that mirror the old ache.

But now – we begin to untie. We begin to see. We begin to heal.

TWO

The Marriage That Shaped Me

When I entered marriage, I thought I was stepping into safety. I thought I had earned a happy ending — or at least a quiet middle. I was young, hopeful, and deeply convinced that if I gave enough, everything would be okay.

But marriage didn't soften me. It stretched me. It made me grow up in silence. It made me hold everything alone — the emotions, the responsibilities, the pain.

It was a relationship where I shrank quietly while smiling publicly. I lost my laughter first, then my voice, and slowly, parts of myself I didn't even realise I had placed on a shelf just to make it work. I thought love was meant to be patient, and so I became endlessly patient. I thought love was sacrifice, and so I bled quietly for years.

The cracks weren't always loud. They showed up in everyday moments – the lack of curiosity about my inner world, the dismissiveness, the absence disguised as presence. But the worst part wasn't what was said. It was what was never said. It was the silence – thick, cold, and never-ending.

I had become a version of myself I no longer recognised – calm on the outside, crumbling on the inside. I was doing everything right, and yet I felt invisible.

When it ended, it felt like I had failed. But in truth, I had simply let go of something that had long stopped holding me. Divorce wasn't my downfall. It was my beginning. It was the first time I chose myself.

Leaving wasn't easy – not in a world that still sees a woman's worth in her ability to hold a marriage together. But it was necessary. Because staying would have meant losing myself completely.

That marriage shaped me, not just through its pain, but through the quiet power I found in walking away. It taught me that love should never cost you your voice. And that peace, even when lonely, is better than chaos that's shared.

But I want to be honest – that marriage also taught me a lot. It brought lessons I couldn't have learnt any other way. It taught me that love, though essential, is not always enough. It woke me from the fairytale I was conditioned to believe in – that marriage would complete me, that once I found a partner, life would be whole.

Instead, I found that I had to complete myself.

Through that marriage, I learned resilience, responsibility, and the strength that comes from standing alone. My ex-husband, despite the differences that led us apart, is someone I now respect deeply. He is a good human being, and I honour the chapter we shared. It made me who I am.

It was during the separation that I began to turn inward – seeking healing, seeking answers. I was introduced to new paths – healing modalities, therapy, spiritual practices. I met people who held space for me, who reflected my worth back to me when I couldn't see it for myself.

That pain was a portal. That ending was an opening. That loss became my teacher.

This chapter is for every woman who stayed too long. Who gave too much. Who believed that loving harder would save it. Sometimes the bravest thing we do is leave – and sometimes, that's when we finally come home to ourselves.

THREE

Motherhood and the Mirror of Love

Becoming a mother changed everything – and nothing – all at once.

I remember the first time I held my child. The world went quiet. My fears paused. For a moment, I was just a woman cradling new life, unaware that this small being would teach me more about love, surrender, and resilience than anyone ever had.

When I became a mother, I believed somewhere deep down that maybe now everything would be okay in my marriage. That this new beginning would bring us closer. But instead, it exposed the distance we had been avoiding. We had different parenting styles, different values, different emotional responses. Instead of binding us, it revealed how far apart we were.

I'm not a perfect mother. And I know my child has had to navigate emotional storms that no child should face. But I tried. I showed up. I did the best I could with the resources I had – emotionally, physically, spiritually.

This isn't about blame. I'm not here to blame anyone, including myself. This is just my journey – raw, real, and full of learning.

My child has been my biggest strength and my deepest source of support. He has seen it all, felt it all, and through it all – we've stood together. We've laughed through the chaos, cried through the pain, and held each other when everything else fell apart.

Motherhood taught me that unconditional love exists. That it isn't grand or loud – it's in the way you wake up tired and still make breakfast. In the way you pause your own breakdown to soothe theirs. In the way their pain hurts more than your own.

Motherhood revealed both the cracks and the strength within me. It showed me the pieces I still needed to heal. It mirrored the parts of me I hadn't faced – my triggers, my tenderness, my fears of abandonment, my need for control. In my son's eyes, I saw my own childhood reappear – and with it, the longing to do better, to love better.

But parenting alone wasn't part of the dream. It was a reality I grew into – not with ease, but with grace. It asked more of me than I knew I had. It forced me to become softer and stronger, often at the same time. It demanded my presence in moments when all I wanted was to escape. And it taught me that sometimes, strength looks like crying in the bathroom, then wiping your face and showing up anyway.

There were days I felt I wasn't enough. When I questioned everything – my choices, my parenting, my worth. But then came the small hands wrapped around mine, the laughter echoing through silence, the unexpected "I love you, Mama," that stitched my heart back together.

In raising my child, I began to reparent myself. I started to notice how my old wounds showed up in the way I responded — the urgency for perfection, the fear of failure, the need for validation. Slowly, gently, I began to offer myself what I was trying to offer him: patience, love, forgiveness.

Being a single mother has been my deepest responsibility and my deepest joy. It stripped away the illusions and brought me face-to-face with truth. It made me financially, emotionally, and spiritually stronger. It made me protect my peace more fiercely. And it brought into sharp focus what kind of love I wanted for myself and my child.

Motherhood didn't just stretch my body. It stretched my soul.

This chapter is for every mother doing the quiet work of holding it all together — not perfectly, but wholeheartedly. It's for the moments no one applauds, for the invisible labor, for the nights spent worrying, and the mornings that begin too early.

And it's a reminder that your love — flawed, fierce, and fully human — is enough.

FOUR

Pillars of My Healing

After the chaos of separation and the deep, demanding rhythm of motherhood, I found grounding in the places I least expected. Not in a new romance, but in my roots. In the quiet strength of my family. In the unwavering support of a few who never let me forget who I was.

My father — steady, present, and kind — became more than just a parent. He became a co-parent to my child, a shield when I felt exposed, a guide when I was lost. He never needed to say much. His presence said it all. Through every breakdown, every challenge, every silence I didn't know how to break, he stood by me. His quiet belief in me became the foundation I didn't know I needed.

My sister — fierce and gentle — held space for me in ways only a sister can. There were days we argued, days we didn't understand each other, but she always came back with warmth. She listened even when I made no sense. She reminded me that even in my mess, I was still worthy of love.

My mother – though our bond had its wounds – showed up in her own ways. There were moments of distance, but also moments of closeness, unexpected care, soft gestures that reached me when I wasn't even looking. And in her own way, she loved. And sometimes, that's all we can ask for.

My friends – a chosen circle of souls – held me when I couldn't hold myself. They listened to the same stories on repeat. They answered late-night messages. They sat with my silence. They never made me feel like I was too much. They showed me what it meant to be truly seen.

And always, always – my Allah. The one constant when everything else changed. I never stopped praying. No matter how broken I felt, there was always the prayer mat. A space where tears were welcomed. Where healing began. Where surrender didn't mean weakness – it meant trust. My faith gave me breath when life felt breathless. It reminded me that I was never alone.

This chapter isn't about struggle – it's about support. It's about the hands that held me, the shoulders I leaned on, the eyes that saw me when I was invisible to myself. It's about the love that came not in grand gestures, but in the form of patience, presence, and prayer.

Sometimes, healing begins not with answers, but with people who sit beside your questions. And I had that. In blood, in friendship, and in faith.

This chapter is for the ones who stayed. Who made tea. Who picked up the phone. Who prayed for me without telling me. Who reminded me of my strength when I forgot.

This is for my family – imperfect, real, and deeply mine.

This is for the quiet miracles that held me together.

FIVE

Choosing Myself

There comes a point in your journey where the loudest voice you need to hear is your own. Not the one that's been conditioned to please, adjust, or shrink – but the one that quietly whispers what you truly need.

For a long time, I thought choosing myself was selfish. I thought love meant constantly making space for someone else, even when I was left with none. I believed that if I just gave more – more patience, more silence, more understanding – eventually, things would feel whole. But I learned that giving too much without receiving is not love. It is abandonment of self, disguised as loyalty.

I stayed in situations because I loved. I forgave because I hoped. I adjusted because I feared loss. And I thought that holding on meant strength – but sometimes, real strength is in letting go of what depletes you, even if you still love it.

Choosing myself didn't come from a place of anger or revenge. It came from exhaustion. From seeing my reflection dim in the mirror. From realizing that my needs matter too – emotional availability, presence, shared dreams, shared effort. And if someone cannot meet me there, I no longer try to build the bridge alone.

It took me years to understand that my peace is sacred. That love shouldn't leave me questioning my worth. That the right relationship feels like home – not like walking on eggshells. Choosing myself meant creating boundaries, not walls. It meant asking myself hard questions: *Does this relationship honor me? Am I heard? Do I feel safe?*

Sometimes the answer hurt. But it also set me free.

Choosing myself meant waking up and not waiting for someone else to show up first. It meant being whole in my own presence, being a mother who's not emotionally drained, being a woman who reclaims softness not from someone else's affection but from her own healing.

It meant redefining love – not as sacrifice, but as mutuality. Not as survival, but as serenity.

And perhaps the most radical act of all? Choosing myself quietly. Not with announcements or ultimatums. But with graceful detachment. With calm. With clarity. With faith that if something is meant for me, it will never ask me to betray myself to keep it.

SIX

Healing Gently

Healing doesn't come like a thunderstorm. It arrives like morning light – quiet, slow, and persistent.

There was a time when I thought healing meant "fixing" – that I had to rush toward becoming better, stronger, happier. But I realized healing is not a race. It's a soft returning – to myself, to God, to peace.

Meditation was one of the first things that held me. In silence, I met the parts of me I had ignored. I watched my breath, my thoughts, my ache – and slowly, I began to feel safer within myself. It wasn't about becoming calm instantly. It was about showing up daily, even when I was broken, even when I cried through the stillness.

And somewhere along the way, I stopped seeking answers outside. I turned inward and upward.

My Lord – He was always there. But in my healing, I found Him again. In every sajdah, I poured my confusion, my pain, my longing. I didn't always get what I asked for, but I always received what I needed: grounding, hope, and love that never abandoned me.

It was through this connection that I realized – I don't have to control everything. My job is to show up with sincerity. The rest? I hand over to Him.

Work became another anchor. Fall honey was not just a business – it was healing in a jar. As I built something with purpose, I rebuilt myself. Creating, nurturing, growing – it gave my pain direction, my emptiness some meaning. Every order packed with love reminded me that I still had something to offer to the world, and to myself.

And then there were my friends – not always many, but the right ones. The ones who didn't need explanations. Who held space for me, sometimes in silence. Who reminded me of who I was when I forgot. We laughed, cried, and rebuilt each other.

Eventually, I reached a point where I no longer needed control to feel safe. I stopped trying to force clarity. I let go of the timeline, the should-haves, the constant questioning. I allowed life to unfold. I began to trust – myself, my journey, and the divine wisdom behind what was withheld and what was given.

Healing, I learned, is not becoming someone else. It's remembering who I've always been, beneath the hurt.

SEVEN

Redefining Love

Love, as I once knew it, was filled with conditions. It was proving, pleasing, holding on – even when I was the only one holding. It was chasing presence, interpreting silences, justifying absences. I confused love with effort, with sacrifice, with making things work.

But healing changed everything. It stripped away the noise and made me ask – *what is love, really?*

Love, I learned, isn't always fireworks or constant reassurance. It is presence. It is peace. It is two people showing up for each other, not out of need, but from choice. Love is not what someone says – it's how they hold you when words fail. It's not dramatic declarations – it's gentle consistency.

I began to realize that love that costs your peace is too expensive.

I once stayed because I believed love should endure anything. But now I know – love should not endure neglect, silence, or emotional absence. Love should not feel like guessing, proving, or waiting in loneliness.

I started paying attention not just to how someone made me feel in their best moments – but how they made me feel in their ordinary ones. Was I safe? Was I seen? Was I respected? Did I feel like a person or a placeholder?

I redefined love – as mutual energy, as partnership, as something that grows with care, not clings with fear. I redefined it as choosing each other daily, with presence, words, and effort. I redefined it as truth – even if that truth means walking away sometimes.

Most of all, I began to give myself the love I once begged for.

The way I talked to myself. The way I paused when I was overwhelmed. The way I stopped chasing people who made me feel hard to love. That, too, was love. Real, grounding, healing love.

And maybe – just maybe – when love comes again, I'll meet it differently. Not from lack. But from fullness. From peace. From clarity. Not to be saved, but to share.

EIGHT

Amaan – My Anchor, My Light

In the middle of everything — the chaos, the pain, the questioning — there was one constant: Amaan.

Becoming a mother didn't fix everything in my marriage, though a part of me quietly hoped it would. But what it did give me was clarity — a purpose so strong that it held me through the darkest nights.

Amaan saw me — not just as a mother, but as a woman navigating heartbreak, healing, and hope. He saw my tears, my strength, my silence. And somehow, even in his little ways, he understood. We've laughed when there was nothing to laugh about. We've hugged when words didn't reach. We've grown up together — I as a woman, he as my son.

He learnt to navigate through emotions early – maybe too early. I wish I could have protected him from it all, but life had other plans. And yet, he rose through it with a grace that surprises me even today. He learnt to read the pauses in my voice, the tiredness in my eyes. Sometimes, he would quietly sit next to me, wordless – offering presence over advice. Other times, he would burst into laughter at the smallest thing, reminding me that joy still lived in the room.

We became each other's safe space. When the world didn't make sense, we returned to our little bubble – dinner conversations, shared glances, random hugs. There was a language between us that no one else spoke. A silent understanding built from being each other's witness.

There were days I felt I wasn't enough. That I wasn't giving him the perfect family, the perfect home, the perfect version of me. But then he would look at me with trust in his eyes, and I'd remind myself – *love is enough.* Presence is enough. Trying is enough.

He became my mirror. When I wanted to give up, I'd look at him and remember why I started again. He reminded me to stay soft, even when life tried to harden me. He gave my pain a purpose, my healing a direction.

In raising Amaan, I was also raising myself – to be stronger, kinder, more honest. He taught me patience. He taught me humor. He taught me that no matter how much I hurt, I still had love to give.

He is the reason I chose to rise, again and again.

Being a single mother is not easy. It's lonely, overwhelming, exhausting. But it's also sacred. It's a bond that no one else understands. A journey of resilience, of growth, of unconditional love.

Amaan doesn't even know how much he's saved me — but one day, I will tell him. That in this wide, uncertain world, he was my safest place. My home. My light.

NINE

The Stories I Heard

After I walked through my own storms, something shifted. I stopped seeing relationships just as personal events in my life, and started seeing them as patterns – emotional landscapes we carry, repeat, and sometimes don't even know we are stuck inside.

It was after my own heartbreaks and healing that I began to truly listen – not just hear words, but feel the weight behind them. Conversations unfolded unexpectedly. Sometimes with close friends. Sometimes with strangers. Sometimes during long drives, quiet dinners, or over a simple cup of chai. And each story revealed something – not just about love or betrayal, but about longing, fear, and survival.

Some women said, *"They never really valued me."*

Others confessed, *"I gave so much, and ended up with almost nothing. I don't even know who I am anymore."*

And some men – softer than they were allowed to show – whispered, *"She wasn't really there. She stayed married to her parents, not to me."*

Or, *"I tried. I worked hard. But I was always the villain in her story."*

That's when I realized – this isn't just about women. Yes, women carry deep emotional wounds, often unspoken. But men, too, carry pain – sometimes deeper, because they're never taught how to name it. They carry the burden of always being strong, of never faltering, of not needing care. And that's where the suffering hides.

I met women who over gave – thinking love would be returned in equal measure.
I met men who loved quietly and collapsed silently when they were left behind.
I met people in marriages where the paper remained, but the heart had long left.
I met those who stayed just for the children – counting days like sacrifices.

And those who longed for a simple thing: to be seen.

Some stayed for love.
Some stayed for safety.
Some stayed out of duty.
Some left for survival.

And some left – but never really moved on.

What people want isn't always the same –

Some longed for physical intimacy, to feel desired again.
Some wanted emotional closeness, to be truly understood.
Some were simply tired of being invisible.

Some wanted financial support, respect, companionship, or relief from loneliness.

And some just wanted to rest — to not have to fight anymore.

No one wants to feel like a burden. No one wants to fail at love. But we often do — not because we're bad people, but because we're broken in places we never knew existed. And those wounds show up in love, in distance, in anger, in silence.

What struck me most was this: people don't always hurt each other out of cruelty. They hurt because they don't know how else to protect their own pain.

And so I listened. I asked nothing in return. I didn't judge. I wasn't there to fix or advise. I was there to understand. And in those stories — raw, unfinished, tangled — I began to see the bigger picture.

Love is not simple.

People are not simple.

And the relationships we build are often mirrors — reflecting not just who we are, but what we need to heal.

The stories I heard became a thread through my own healing. They reminded me that I was not alone. That what I had felt was not just mine. That this journey of loving, hurting, breaking, and becoming — it's all part of something larger.

This chapter is not about placing blame or drawing conclusions.

It's about witnessing.

It's about starting to ask — not what's wrong with people, but what happened to them? What shaped their fears? What taught them love? And what needs to be unlearned?

And maybe, just maybe, by understanding others, I began to understand myself better too.

Pause & Reflect

Before you turn the page, take a moment to check in with yourself — not as a reader, but as a human who has also lived, loved, lost, and longed.

You, too, carry stories. Some told. Some hidden. Some still unfolding.

✍ **Journal Prompt:**

- Whose story have you never told, not even to yourself?
- What relationship in your life has shaped you the most — and why?
- What have you learned by listening to others without judgment?
- Are there patterns you notice in the stories you hear — or in the ones you keep repeating?

You don't need to write perfect sentences. Let it flow. Be honest. Be gentle. You are not here to fix anything — only to see it clearly.

This is where your own thread of understanding begins.

TEN

Patterns That Repeat

The more I listened to people, the more I realized: it wasn't always about the person they were with. It was about the pattern they were caught in.

She kept choosing emotionally unavailable men — the ones who made her feel like she had to earn love.

He kept falling for women who needed rescuing, because being needed made him feel worthy.

Another clung tightly to someone who treated her like a second option, hoping one day she'd be the first.

And some ran at the first sign of real closeness — because love felt too intense, too unfamiliar, too risky.

Different stories.

Same patterns.

I began to see how we repeat what's familiar, not what's healthy. How many of us aren't chasing love – we're chasing validation. Trying to heal the original wound through someone new, without realizing we're bleeding into every new connection.

We stay where we are anxious, but at least not alone.
We over-function, hoping our love will "fix" what's broken in the other.
We confuse calm with boredom because our nervous system is addicted to chaos.
And the truth is: these patterns are not accidents.

They are *responses* – often unconscious – to something much older.

Somewhere in our early years, we learned what love looked like. For some, love came with conditions. For others, it came and went without warning. Some had to perform to be noticed. Some had to shrink to be safe.

So we carry those templates forward.

The woman who was never heard by her father ends up with a partner who never really listens.

The boy who had to be "strong" for his mother becomes a man who never allows himself to fall apart.

The girl who was constantly compared learns to see love as a competition – where she must outdo, outperform, or prove.

We think we're making new choices, but often, we're just repeating old stories with new characters.

And unless we stop and reflect – we'll keep calling it fate, when it's just a pattern.

But the beautiful thing about patterns is: they can be unlearned.

It begins with awareness.

With asking:

- Why do I react this way?
- Why do I feel safest when I'm not fully seen?
- Why do I chase people who don't choose me?
- Why do I fear love that feels calm?

Patterns aren't punishments. They're clues.

They show us what needs to be healed, what's ready to be released.

And the moment we name them – the moment we see them – we begin to create space for something different.

🖎 ▩ Journal Prompt:

- What patterns do you notice in your romantic or emotional relationships?
- Are there similar types of people you attract – or are drawn to?
- Do you tend to overgive, avoid, shut down, chase, or stay too long?
- Where do you think this began?

Write freely. No edits. No shame. Just awareness. Because awareness is the beginning of choice.

ELEVEN

Attachment Styles – How We Love

As I listened to people share their relationship struggles – the ache of being left, the exhaustion of giving too much, the discomfort of being truly seen – I began to realize something:

We don't all love the same way.

We don't all *fear* the same things in love either.

Some fear being abandoned.
Some fear being consumed.
Some fear not being good enough.
Some fear being truly known.

These fears don't always come from our current relationship.

Often, they come from far before — shaped in the early spaces where love first showed up, or didn't.

That's when I began to learn about **attachment styles.** Not to label people. Not to overthink or diagnose. But to *understand.* To make sense of why so many people — including myself — kept falling into the same emotional loops, even when we wanted something better.

🖇 Anxious Attachment - "Will you stay?"

People with this attachment style often carry a deep, almost invisible fear: *that they will be left.*

Love, for them, is often anxious — full of second-guessing and internal chaos.

They tend to overgive. They check their phones too many times. They read between the lines, replay conversations, and imagine worst-case scenarios. Not because they're dramatic — but because unpredictability triggers old wounds.

They often fall into relationships where they feel like they're the only one trying — hoping that their loyalty will eventually be rewarded. But it rarely is.

Deep down, they don't just want love — they want *reassurance.*

Tell me I matter.
Show me I won't be left.
Make me feel safe.

And until they learn to self-soothe, they often seek this safety in unavailable places.

⌘ Avoidant Attachment – "Don't come too close."

Avoidantly attached people often look confident, independent, in control.

But underneath that is usually someone who learned — early on — that closeness isn't safe.

Maybe their emotions weren't welcomed as a child.
Maybe love was inconsistent, or felt overwhelming.
So they taught themselves: *Don't depend on anyone. Stay guarded.*

When things get emotional, they withdraw. When someone gets too close, they pull away.
They might care deeply but express it in confusing ways — silence, distance, jokes, indifference.

They often choose partners who are more emotionally expressive — and then feel overwhelmed by them.

It becomes a dance of *come close, go away.*

And while they long for love, they fear the vulnerability it requires.

Disorganized Attachment – "I want love, but I don't trust it."

This style carries both anxious and avoidant tendencies.

People with disorganized attachment often grew up in environments where love was mixed with fear or unpredictability.

They may crave closeness — but once they get it, they panic.

They may sabotage healthy relationships and chase the ones that leave them unsettled.

They are often misunderstood — even by themselves.
Why do I keep doing this?
Why do I push people away, then beg them to come back?

This isn't confusion. This is a trauma response.
A nervous system stuck between wanting connection and fearing it.

Disorganized attachment is not a character flaw — it's the result of emotional pain never being processed or soothed.

🌱 Secure Attachment - "I'm here. And I'm not leaving."

Securely attached people aren't perfect — but they're safe.

They can express emotions without shame.
They can give love and receive it.
They're not easily thrown by conflict.
They're not terrified by space or intimacy.

Their love is calm, consistent, and grounded.
They don't need someone to fill a void — because they've already learned how to hold themselves.

Being with someone secure can feel… boring at first. Especially if you're used to chaos.
But give it time — and you'll realize: it's not boring.
It's peace.

We Are Not Fixed

Here's what I want to say most:
You are **not** your attachment style.
You are the awareness underneath it.

We can move.

Anxious can become more secure.
Avoidant can learn to open.
Disorganized can learn to trust.
Secure people, too, can wobble — and come back.

Our styles aren't identities.
They're patterns.
And all patterns can shift — with awareness, compassion, and practice.

The more I learned about this, the more I softened toward myself.
I stopped blaming myself for reacting.
I stopped blaming others too.
We're all just trying to feel safe. We're all trying to love with whatever tools we were given.

But now — we have new ones.

✍ ▩ **Journal Prompt:**

- Which attachment style feels most like you — right now?
- What triggers that style in your relationships?
- How did love feel in your childhood? Were you soothed, dismissed, smothered, ignored?
- How do you want to *love differently* moving forward?

Write slowly. Breathe as you reflect. This isn't about fixing. It's about understanding — and that, already, is healing.

TWELVE

Where It Comes From

No one wakes up one day and decides to fear intimacy.

No one chooses to be clingy, distant, overgiving, guarded, or confused in love.

These patterns — they come from somewhere.

And more often than not, they start early.

Before we had language. Before we had boundaries. Before we knew what to call "love."

To understand how we love as adults, we must gently look back at the first places we learned what love meant — our childhood homes, our caregivers, our environment.

It's not about blame. It's about clarity.

Love Was First a Lesson

If you were loved conditionally – only when you performed, behaved, excelled, or stayed quiet – you might still believe that love must be earned.

If your emotions were too much for the people around you, you may have learned to suppress them. To stay small. To never be a burden.

If affection was absent, inconsistent, or confusing, you may now crave closeness yet fear it. You may chase unavailable love because it mirrors what you once called home.

If love came with chaos, criticism, or caretaking – you might now confuse peace with boredom and feel safest in emotional intensity.

We carry these invisible lessons into every relationship – not just romantic ones.

Friendships, parenting, work dynamics – all of them echo our early bonds.

And the truth is, no one had perfect parents.

Many of our caregivers did the best they could with the tools they had.

But that doesn't mean we didn't inherit their fears, silence, absence, or overcontrol.

Becoming Aware of the Origins

Healing began, for me, when I stopped asking:

What's wrong with me?
And instead asked:
Where did this begin?

Why do I shrink when I express a need?
Why do I feel safest when I'm in control?
Why does love scare me more than being alone?

The answers often led back to my inner child — the girl who learned to keep the peace, to over-function, to become what others needed, even when it hurt.

She didn't need fixing.
She needed holding.
And I — the woman I've become — finally chose to hold her.

Breaking the Generational Loop

When we don't pause to reflect, we pass down what hurt us.
We can unconsciously become the emotionally distant parent we once longed to reach.
We can mirror the control we rebelled against.
We can raise children in a home that feels just like the one we were trying to heal from.

But the moment we become conscious — the loop starts to loosen.

Every moment of awareness is a doorway:
To parent ourselves with more kindness.
To love others without re-enacting our wounds.
To forgive, not to forget, but to free.

This chapter is not about digging through pain just for the sake of it.
It's about *naming things*, so they no longer control us in silence.

Because the moment you see where it comes from,
is the moment you begin to choose something different.

✍️ 🟩 Journal Prompt:

- What early experiences shaped your view of love, trust, and connection?
- How were emotions handled in your childhood – were they welcomed or dismissed?
- Did you feel like you had to earn love, stay perfect, or disappear to feel safe?
- What patterns from your past might still be influencing your present?

Write gently. This is sacred work. You're not blaming the past – you're reclaiming your future.

THIRTEEN

Healing Our Patterns

Once you see the pattern, you can't unsee it.
And at first, that can feel overwhelming.
You might wonder – *Have I been repeating this all my life?*
You might feel guilt, grief, even shame.
But let me tell you something: awareness is not a burden.
It's a breakthrough.

Patterns are not proof that you're broken.
They are signs that something inside you wants attention.
Wants safety.
Wants to choose differently – this time, consciously.

The First Step: Pause Before You React

Healing doesn't mean you'll never get triggered.
It means you'll start recognizing when you're triggered – and

learn to pause.
That pause is sacred.
It's the space between the old reaction and a new response.
It's where the rewiring begins.

When you're tempted to shut down, chase, fix, or lash out — pause.

Breathe.

Ask yourself: *Is this coming from my wound or my wisdom?*

Even just noticing is a powerful shift.

Become Curious, Not Critical

Healing isn't linear. You'll repeat patterns. You'll slip. You'll react. That's okay.
Don't shame yourself. *Study yourself.*

Instead of *"What's wrong with me?" ask, "What is this reaction trying to protect me from?"*
Instead of *"I always mess up," try, "Something inside me still feels unsafe. Let me meet that part with kindness."*

When we treat ourselves with curiosity instead of criticism, healing becomes sustainable — not something we push through, but something we soften into.

Reparenting the Inner Child

Most patterns are echoes of childhood needs that were unmet.
The child who wasn't chosen.
The child who had to earn love.
The child who was invisible, or too responsible, or never safe.
That child still lives in us — and shows up in our relationships.

Reparenting means becoming the adult you needed.
Offering yourself what no one else did.

Try this in your journaling or meditation:

- *"What did I need to hear as a child that I never did?"*
- *"How can I offer that to myself now?"*

Sometimes, healing is as simple as saying: *"You are safe now. I've got you."*

Choosing Differently, Even When It's Hard

You won't always feel ready to break the pattern – but you can still choose differently.

- Say "no" when your old self would've said "yes" to be loved.
- Speak up, even if your voice shakes.
- Allow love in, even if part of you wants to run.
- Let someone go, even if you love them, because they do not love you well.

Each time you do this – you build new emotional muscles.
Each time, you prove to your nervous system: *It is safe to love differently. It is safe to be me.*

Healing is not just about who you let in.
It's about who you choose to become in the process.

Small Daily Practices That Help

- **Daily check-ins:** "What am I feeling right now?"
- **Self-touch:** Place your hand on your heart or stomach. Breathe slowly. Calm your body.

- **Affirmations that speak directly to your wound:**
  "I do not have to earn love."
  "I am safe without controlling everything."
  "My worth is not dependent on how others treat me."
- **Therapy, journaling, prayer, nature, music** – anything that brings you back to yourself.

You don't need to be perfect. You just need to be present.

Journal Prompt:

- What reactions or relationship patterns are you ready to start shifting?
- What would the healed version of you do in those moments?
- What is one loving action you can take this week toward that version of you?

Be gentle. You are not late. You are not failing.

You are learning how to love – again, and this time, fully awake.

FOURTEEN

What Love Can Look Like

For a long time, I thought love had to hurt a little.
That it had to involve waiting, chasing, proving.
That love meant adjusting, tolerating, enduring.

But healing taught me something else.
Love – real love – doesn't feel like a test.
It feels like a place to rest.

Once we understand our patterns and begin to see clearly, we realize that many of the things we once called love… were actually longing, survival, or familiarity.
And when that realization lands, we start asking:
If not that – then what does love truly look like?

Love Can Look Like Peace

Not silence as punishment.
Not holding your breath, waiting for their mood to shift.

But quiet mornings. Unforced conversations. Being together without tension.

Love can be **calm.**
It doesn't need to constantly spark. Sometimes, it simply glows.

Love Can Look Like Effort

Not grand gestures once in a while – but consistency.
Checking in. Showing up. Making space for each other.
Not as obligation, but as choice.

Effort in real love isn't exhausting. It's nourishing.
It says, *"You matter to me, even on my busy days."*

💬 Love Can Look Like Being Seen

Love listens. Love asks. Love remembers.
Love doesn't make you shrink to fit its comfort.
It stretches to make space for your voice, your truth, your past, your dreams.

Love says, *"You don't have to pretend. I see you – and I still choose you."*

Love Can Look Like Boundaries

Love doesn't mean losing yourself.
In fact, true love respects individuality.
It says, *"I want to grow with you, not consume you."*

There's room to breathe, to be, to evolve – both together and apart.

Love Can Look Like Healing

In the presence of the right kind of love, old wounds rise – not to ruin, but to be seen and soothed.

A healthy relationship may not be free of triggers, but it becomes a safe place to bring them.

Love holds your hand while you work through your fear — not shames you for having it.

Love Can Look Like Choosing Yourself Too

The best kind of love doesn't replace your relationship with yourself — it deepens it.

In healthy love, you don't lose your identity.

You rediscover it — stronger, fuller, more alive.

Love is not about becoming one.

It's about being whole beside another whole.

I used to think love had to be dramatic.

Now I know — love can be simple.

Soft. Steady. Secure.

And that doesn't make it less passionate.

It makes it *sustainable.*

✍ ▩ Journal Prompt:

- What did you once believe love should feel like?
- What beliefs are you now ready to release?
- What does healthy, peaceful, mutual love look like to you — emotionally, physically, spiritually?
- Can you imagine giving yourself that kind of love, starting today?

You are not too much.

You are not too late.

You are just beginning to love yourself in the way you always deserved to be loved.

FIFTEEN

Coming Home to Ourselves

After all the stories, patterns, heartbreaks, lessons, and healing, we often arrive at a place we didn't expect:

Ourselves.

We come full circle – not with a perfect relationship, or a partner who ticks every box, or a life without any wounds – but with a deeper understanding of who we are beneath it all.

That's what this journey has been about.

Not fixing.
Not forgetting.
But *returning*.

Returning to the part of us that always knew:
"I am worthy of love that does not confuse me."
"I do not need to shrink to be chosen."

"I am allowed to want connection – and peace."

"I am allowed to say no."

"I am enough."

💞 The Real Relationship Is the One You Have With Yourself

When you begin to meet your own needs – emotionally, spiritually, even physically – you stop chasing love like it's a lifeline.

You stop begging.

You stop performing.

You stop staying in spaces where your silence is more welcomed than your voice.

You begin to choose differently – from clarity, not fear.

You begin to see red flags not as puzzles to solve, but as signs to pause.

You begin to honor yourself – not in rebellion, but in remembrance.

Because the most sacred relationship you will ever have is the one with your own heart.

Coming Home Feels Like...

- Speaking kindly to yourself.
- Trusting your body's signals.
- Creating boundaries that don't require apology.
- Finding joy in solitude.
- Holding space for your own grief – and not rushing it.
- Letting go without losing yourself.
- Choosing peace over drama, clarity over confusion, softness over survival.

Coming home isn't loud.

It's a quiet realization that you no longer need to be found – you were never lost.

✍ ▩ Final Reflection:

- What part of yourself are you finally ready to come home to?
- What belief, relationship, or story are you ready to release?
- What kind of love do you now want to cultivate – within and around you?
- If you were to write a love letter to yourself, what would it say?

Write it.

Read it.

Live it.

Because you are not a half looking for another half.

You are already whole.

And now, you're finally home.

Part : Practices for the Heart

Tools for Healing, Reflecting, and Loving with Clarity

This part of the book isn't about theory. It's about action – quiet, meaningful action.

Healing doesn't always happen in big decisions. Often, it begins in the small moments we choose to pause, breathe, listen, and show up differently – for ourselves.

You don't need to do all these practices at once.
You don't need to be perfect with them.
All you need is *presence.*

These practices are here to help you return – again and again – to the love within.

Practice 1: The Daily Check-In

Every day, ask yourself:

- What am I feeling right now?
- What part of me needs attention or kindness?
- Am I trying to control, avoid, or numb something?

Close your eyes. Breathe deeply for a minute. Listen without fixing.

This is how you learn to respond, not react. To love, not abandon yourself.

Practice 2: A Love Letter to Yourself

Write a letter to yourself as if you were someone who loves you unconditionally.

Include:

- What you admire about yourself
- What you forgive yourself for
- What you're proud of
- What you promise yourself going forward

Read it back on difficult days. Let it remind you of who you are beyond fear.

🧸 Practice 3: Inner Child Dialogue

Find a quiet moment. Picture your younger self – age 5, 7, or 10.

Ask:

- What were you feeling back then?
- What did you need but never received?
- What would you like to say to that younger version of you?

Now write a short note to that child, ending with:

"You are safe now. I'm here with you."

Practice 4: Pattern Mapping

Take a sheet of paper and draw a timeline of your past relationships – romantic or otherwise.

For each one, reflect:

- How did it start?
- How did it make you feel?
- What pattern do you notice now?
- What part of you was choosing from fear or survival?

This isn't to blame yourself. It's to bring awareness – so your next chapter begins with choice, not habit.

SIXTEEN

The Guilt of Leaving

Some grief doesn't come from being left – it comes from choosing to leave. From being the one who walks away. From being the woman who decides, after years of hoping, adjusting, and quietly breaking – to stop trying.

We don't talk enough about this kind of grief. The one wrapped in guilt. The one that keeps you up at night wondering:

"Did I try hard enough?"
"Did I give up too soon?"
"What about the children?"
"What will people say?"

We live in a world where endurance is glorified. Especially for women. You're applauded for how long you can hold on, how much pain you can carry in silence, how well you can smile through the storm. But rarely are you celebrated for leaving. Even when leaving is the bravest thing you'll ever do.

I've met women who stayed in relationships that drained them emotionally, physically, spiritually. They stayed because they were taught that marriage is forever. That leaving is shameful. That sacrificing yourself is love. They stayed for the children. For the families. For the image. For fear of loneliness.

But eventually, something inside them whispered — **"Enough."**

One woman I met had been married for ten years. Her husband never raised his hand but constantly silenced her spirit. He never shouted, but his silence was louder than anything. She was told by everyone that she had a perfect life. But inside the walls of her home, she felt invisible. Forgotten. Alone.

She left. Not in rage — but in quiet sorrow.
And still, she carried guilt.
Especially for her children.

"Did I break their home?" she asked.

But over time, she realised something powerful — staying would have taught them that love means **shrinking yourself.**

Another woman I met left a relationship where she gave everything — her time, her body, her heart, her dreams. She waited for him to meet her halfway. But he never showed up. She finally left. And then came the sadness.

Not because she missed him — but because she had lost the version of herself who still believed she could fix everything with enough love.

But the story that stayed with me the most was of a woman who left after 32 years of marriage.

She had it all — in the eyes of the world. A big home. Financial security. Adult children. Social respect.

But inside, she was alone. Emotionally, mentally, spiritually. She told me, "I lived with him like a well-behaved ghost."

She left quietly. With no drama. Just the decision to finally choose herself.

And even then, she whispered to me, **"Do you think I failed?"**

I looked at her — her grace, her courage — and said, **"No. You lived. You finally chose to live."**

The guilt of leaving is heavy. It's shaped by stories passed down through generations — stories that tell us endurance is noble, and that self-abandonment is the price of love.

But here's what I want you to know:

Leaving is not failure.
It is not betrayal.
It is not selfish.

To anyone carrying that guilt — I see you.

You did not walk away because you stopped loving.

You walked away because you started remembering **you deserve to be loved too** — deeply, fully, without being erased in the process.

Leaving is not the opposite of loyalty.
Sometimes, it is the most sacred act of loyalty — to yourself, to your children, to your soul.
Sometimes, it is the loudest "I choose me" in a world that taught you not to.

Let that be your truth.

Reflection for the Reader: Releasing the Guilt

Take a quiet moment. Breathe deeply. Sit with yourself.

Now ask:

- Did I ever feel guilty for wanting to leave something that hurt me?
- What stories have I inherited about staying and sacrificing?
- If I imagined my daughter or best friend in the same situation – would I ask her to stay?

Sometimes, we are kinder to others than to ourselves.

Write freely in response to these:

1. **What did I lose by staying too long?**
2. **What did I fear I'd lose if I left?**
3. **What part of me whispered "leave" long before I actually did?**
4. **Can I forgive myself for not leaving sooner – or for having to leave at all?**

And finally:

What would it mean to let go of the guilt and walk into grace?

SEVENTEEN

Loneliness in Togetherness

There's a kind of loneliness that doesn't come from being alone.
It comes from lying next to someone who feels miles away.
From eating dinner across the table in silence.
From sharing a home but not a heart.

This is the loneliness of togetherness – and it's one of the hardest to explain.
Because on the outside, everything looks "fine."
But on the inside, there's a growing emptiness, like living in a house that used to feel like home, but now echoes instead.

I met a woman who said, "I miss him even when he's right here."
He wasn't cruel. He wasn't absent. But he was... disconnected. Present in body. Absent in soul.
She longed for a conversation that didn't feel like obligation.
She longed for a touch that wasn't routine.
She longed to be seen, not just looked at.

Loneliness in togetherness is subtle. It creeps in slowly.
It starts with shorter conversations.
Then fewer shared moments.
Then separate emotional worlds.
Until one day you realise – **you've stopped trying to reach each other at all.**

What makes this kind of loneliness painful is the shame that often comes with it.

"How can I feel lonely? I'm not alone."
We question ourselves. We suppress the ache.
We perform normalcy for the world – and sometimes, even for ourselves.
But here's the truth:

You can feel abandoned without being left.

You can crave connection in the presence of someone you love.
You can be deeply lonely… even in a relationship.

And it's not your fault.

This loneliness is not a weakness. It's your soul calling for intimacy. For attention. For life.
Some stay. Some choose to talk. Some choose to leave.
But whatever path you choose, it begins with this: **honesty with yourself.**

Ask yourself:

- When did I last feel seen?
- Do I miss who we were – or do I miss who I was, before I started fading?
- Have I been performing connection instead of feeling it?

You deserve a love that looks at you and says: "I see you. I'm here. Let's meet again."

Reflection for the Reader: Naming the Quiet Ache

Take a moment. Let the silence speak.

Now ask yourself:

1. **Have I ever felt lonely in the presence of someone I loved?**
2. **What were the signs I was emotionally drifting – or being emotionally abandoned?**
3. **Did I stop asking for what I needed because I was tired... or afraid of the answer?**
4. **Did we grow apart, or did I shrink to survive the silence?**

And then, write freely in response to this:

If I could speak to the version of me that felt invisible in that relationship, what would I say to her now?

EIGHTEEN

Love, Loss, and the Body

Some heartbreaks don't start in the heart — they start in the body.

The shallow breath.
The lump in your throat that stays for days.
The ache in your chest that arrives quietly every night.
The way your hands tremble after a fight.
The way your stomach tightens when you're trying to be okay.

We are taught to talk about love with our minds and grieve with our words — but rarely are we told:

Your body remembers.

Every silence. Every goodbye. Every act of abandonment — it settles somewhere in the body.
In the tightness of your shoulders.
In the fatigue that no amount of sleep can fix.
In the tears that show up when you finally sit still.

I met a woman who said,

"After he left, I couldn't eat for weeks. My body literally shut down. I couldn't even swallow water without feeling a wave of grief."

It wasn't just about the breakup.

It was about the energy of loss – and how her body had been holding in that ache long before the relationship ended.

Another woman told me,

"Every time I heard his car in the driveway, I'd tense up. I thought I was anxious – but now I know, my body was reacting to years of emotional unpredictability."

The body doesn't lie.

It stores what the heart tries to forget.

It carries the burden when the mind can't make sense of the chaos.

But here's the beautiful part:

The body also knows how to heal.

Through movement.

Through breath.

Through rest.

Through safe touch.

Through softness.

You can't think your way out of heartbreak – but you can **breathe** your way through it.

You can walk. Cry. Stretch. Shake. Dance.

You can place your hand on your chest and say, "I'm here."

You can learn to feel safe in your skin again.

Because healing is not just emotional. It is physical.

It is cellular.

It is spiritual.

So today, ask yourself:

- Where in my body am I still carrying the weight of what I've lived through?
- What does my body need to release that my words haven't said?
- Can I give myself permission to listen, without fixing?

Sometimes, the most radical thing you can do is **return to your body** – gently, slowly, with love.

Practice: Coming Home to Your Body

This is not a workout.
This is not a ritual.
This is a remembering.
You are safe. You are here. You are allowed to feel.

✯ Step 1: Find a Quiet Space

Sit or lie down in a comfortable, quiet space. Let your spine rest gently – upright or reclined. Allow your hands to fall open. Close your eyes if it feels safe.

✯ Step 2: Anchor Into Breath

Place one hand on your heart, one on your belly.
Inhale slowly through your nose – feel your belly rise.
Exhale gently through your mouth – feel your body soften.
Repeat this **4-5 times,** letting each breath be a little deeper, a little slower.

✯ Step 3: Scan and Soften

Bring your attention to your body from head to toe.

Say to yourself gently as you move through each area:

- "I release the weight from my forehead."
- "I soften my jaw."
- "I let go of tension in my shoulders."
- "I breathe into my chest."
- "I send kindness to my belly."
- "I allow my legs to rest."

There is no rush. Your body will meet you where you are.

✯ Step 4: Emotional Movement (Optional)

If it feels natural – sway your upper body gently.
Roll your shoulders.
Stretch your arms.
Let a sound out if it wants to come.
Tears are welcome. Stillness is welcome.
This is your body speaking.

✯ Step 5: Loving Touch

Wrap your arms around yourself like a hug.
Whisper softly:

"I'm here. I've got you. You're safe now."

Feel your own warmth.
Stay in this embrace for as long as you need.

✯ Step 6: Close with Gratitude

When you're ready, place your hands in prayer or on your heart.

Thank your body for surviving, for holding you, for never giving up on you.

Repeat this practice anytime you feel disconnected, overwhelmed, or heavy with emotion.

Your healing doesn't have to be loud.

Your body is a sacred space — let it guide you home.

NINETEEN

The Love I Gave Away

Somewhere along the way, many of us learned to love by giving.
By proving.
By fixing.
By becoming so useful, so nurturing, so available – that we were impossible to leave.

But love that demands you disappear is not love.
Love that thrives only when you overextend is not love.
And yet – how many times have we done it?

I once sat across from a woman who said,
"I don't know how to receive. I only know how to give."
She had loved deeply – with gestures, time, sacrifice. But when she looked back, she realised:

No one had ever stayed for her.
They stayed for what she did.

Another woman told me,
"I felt guilty resting. Like I had to earn love every single day."
She had turned love into labor – into a checklist, a race, a ritual of performance.
And when it wasn't returned, she didn't question the balance.
She questioned her worth.

This chapter is for the woman who kept giving long after she ran out.
Who poured from an empty cup.
Who believed that her love would fix everything – if she just gave more.
This chapter is for the woman who over functioned in the relationship... and now wonders why she feels so tired.

Let's be clear: **Your love is beautiful.**
But love is not a transaction.
It is not a tool to keep someone beside you.
It is not a weapon you use on yourself.

You do not have to earn the right to be loved.
You do not have to perform your way into someone's heart.
You deserve to be held – not because you are strong, or generous, or forgiving – but because you are human.

Let this be the beginning of reclaiming the love you gave away.
Not with regret.
But with grace.

Let it return to you –
as rest,
as boundaries,
as softness,
as peace

Reflection + Practice: Reclaiming My Love

Find a quiet moment with yourself. Light a candle if it feels right. Keep your journal nearby. Breathe.

Then ask:

1. Where did I learn that I have to give to be loved?

Was it in childhood? In my first relationship? In marriage? In motherhood?

2. What did I give that no one noticed — but I still remember?

Was it my silence? My time? My dreams?

3. Was there ever a moment I gave more than I received — and blamed myself for it?

Write the memory. Let it rise. Let it breathe.
Now pause.
Close your eyes.
Place both hands on your heart.
And say softly:

"Dear self, I see all the love you gave. I honor it. I return it to you now. Not in bitterness, but in warmth. You do not have to prove anything to be worthy of love."

Bonus Practice: The Receiving Ritual

Each day this week, do **one act of receiving:**

- Let someone help you.
- Rest without guilt.
- Say yes to kindness.
- Say no without explaining.

And when it feels hard, remind yourself:

"I am allowed to receive the kind of love I always gave."

TWENTY

Who Am I Without Them?

When a relationship ends — especially one that shaped your daily life, your choices, your future — it's not just the person you lose.

You lose the version of **yourself** you became inside that relationship.

Suddenly, the routines feel empty.

The bed feels too big.

You walk into a room and forget what you came for.

You reach for your phone out of habit — and then remember there's no one to message.

But beneath all of that, a deeper question starts to rise:

Who am I now?

What do I like, want, believe — without them?

What's left of me when I'm not someone's partner, someone's anchor, someone's emotional caretaker?

I met a woman who said,
"After the divorce, I didn't know what to order at restaurants. Everything I used to order was what *he* liked."
She had curated her preferences around his. Her identity had fused with his routines, his needs, his rhythms.
And when it all ended, she had to rediscover her own.

Another woman shared,

"I had wrapped my worth in his love. When he left, I felt like I disappeared."
She wasn't grieving *him* as much as she was grieving the self she lost while trying to hold on to the relationship.

And then there was the woman who was just **26** – with two small children – sitting on a one-way flight back to her parents' home in the middle of a divorce.

She stared out the window as the clouds passed, wondering how her life had changed so quickly.

She hadn't worked in years. She didn't know how to restart. She was afraid of judgment, afraid of failing her children, afraid of the silence that would greet her in the middle of the night.

But most of all, she was afraid of herself – or rather, how little she recognized who she was anymore.

That's the thing no one prepares you for.

When the relationship ends, you're not just left with an empty bed.

You're left with an identity you no longer know how to wear.

A version of yourself that existed mostly in response to someone else.

This is the silent grief of separation.
Not the crying. Not the heartbreak.
But the quiet, uncertain becoming.
The discomfort of standing in front of a mirror, unsure of who's looking back.

But here's the beauty:

This space of not knowing — of emptiness — is also the space of **rebirth.**

Of becoming again.

Of asking:

- What do I want now?
- What makes me feel alive?
- What part of me did I silence to keep the peace?

The healing isn't in rushing to fill the void.
It's in learning to sit in the stillness — and listen.
It's in letting go of the identity that was built for someone else's love, and gently building one rooted in your own.

So if you are in that space right now — uncertain, untethered, in-between —
know this:
You are not lost.
You are **returning.**

Reflection Practice: Reclaiming the Forgotten Self

This practice is not about fixing anything.
It's about remembering the woman who existed — and still exists — beneath all the roles, relationships, and responsibilities.
Find a quiet space. Sit with your journal. Breathe gently. Then begin.

✯ Part 1: The Honest Questions

Write freely in response to these:

1. **What parts of myself did I abandon to keep that relationship alive?**
2. **What did I stop doing, wearing, creating, dreaming of – just to be accepted or loved?**
3. **What did I used to love before I became 'someone's person'?**
4. **What would I do today if no one was watching or judging me?**

Let yourself answer without filters. Let the page hold what your voice hasn't spoken.

✯ Part 2: The Mirror Whisper

Stand in front of a mirror. Look into your own eyes. Gently say:

"I'm still here. You are not too late. You are allowed to begin again."

Repeat it until your body believes it.
Place your hand over your heart. Feel it beat. That's proof of life. Of return. Of possibility.

✯ Part 3: A Small Step Forward

Before you close your journal, write one small thing you will do this week – just for you.

- A walk alone in nature
- Dancing in your room
- Cooking your favourite meal
- Wearing something that feels like you

- Revisiting an old hobby
- Saying no without guilt

Because each small act is not just self-care. It's self-return.

TWENTY ONE

Where Our Patterns Come From

No one wakes up one day and decides to overgive.

No one consciously chooses to fear love, or sabotage it, or shrink themselves to fit into someone else's world.

Our patterns didn't begin in our adult relationships.

They were shaped long before – in living rooms filled with unspoken tension, in childhoods where affection had to be earned, in cultures that taught us sacrifice is love and silence is strength.

Some of us were raised to please.

To anticipate needs.

To avoid conflict at all costs.

We learned early on that love came when we were "good," quiet, helpful, or selfless.

Others learned that love meant **earning** – through achievement, responsibility, or emotional labour.
Some of us became the fixers. The caregivers. The ones who always understood, always forgave.

And some – especially men – were never taught how to sit with emotion at all.
They were told: *Don't cry. Be a man. Toughen up.*
So they buried their softness.
And now, when love comes knocking, they don't know how to answer with their full self – because no one ever showed them how.

One woman told me,
"I don't even know how to ask for what I want. I was raised to be grateful with whatever I'm given."
And a man shared,
"I don't talk about my emotions. Not because I don't have them – but because I've never had the language. I was always told it's weakness."

The truth is:

We are all carrying something.

Beliefs. Wounds. Roles. Habits that were once survival tools.
We repeat them – not because we want to stay stuck – but because they feel familiar.

But just because it's familiar doesn't mean it's healthy.
And just because it was passed down doesn't mean we have to pass it forward.

This chapter isn't about blame. It's about awareness.
Because once you see a pattern, you can begin to shift it.

You can pause when you feel the urge to fix.
You can breathe when silence feels safer than truth.
You can catch yourself when you start overgiving — and instead, return to yourself.

Because love doesn't ask us to be perfect.
It asks us to be conscious.
To know where we come from — so we can choose where we go next.

Reflection for Awareness: Tracing the Roots

Find a quiet moment. Sit with yourself — not to fix, but to listen.

Now journal your responses, without judgment:

1. **What was the emotional environment of my childhood home?**

   (Was love freely expressed? Were emotions welcome or silenced?)
2. **What did I learn about love from my parents or primary caregivers?**

   (Did I see love as sacrifice? Control? Distance? Devotion?)
3. **Was I encouraged to express my needs, or did I learn to suppress them?**
4. **What role did I unconsciously play in my early relationships?**

   (The pleaser, the fixer, the quiet one, the strong one...)
5. **How do these patterns show up in my current or past relationships?**

   (Do I overgive, avoid conflict, fear abandonment, struggle to receive?)

A Gentle Reminder:

"I am not to blame for the patterns I inherited – but I am responsible for what I choose to carry forward."

Breathe. Let that land in your heart.

You're not broken. You're becoming conscious.

TWENTY TWO

Building Wholeness, Together

Real relationships are not made of grand gestures and perfect compatibility.
They are made of two people – imperfect, healing, growing – choosing to show up, again and again.

We often enter relationships thinking the other person will complete us.
But the truth is: no one can fill what we refuse to look at.
No one can save us from the work we're meant to do within ourselves.

In a world that romanticizes "finding your other half," we forget – **you were never a half to begin with.**

True partnership isn't about fixing each other.

It's about being safe places for one another's truth.

It's about saying:

"I'm doing my work. You're doing yours. And together, we can build something honest."

One couple I met shared this beautiful insight:

"We used to blame each other for not being enough. But the day we stopped expecting the other to heal our wounds, and started talking about them instead – everything changed."

This is what building wholeness together looks like:

- Taking ownership of your emotions instead of projecting them
- Listening to understand, not just to reply
- Giving space without withdrawing love
- Supporting each other's growth, even when it's uncomfortable
- Learning to sit with discomfort without running
- Celebrating differences instead of fearing them

Balance doesn't mean keeping score.

It means recognising that sometimes one of you will carry more – but it evens out when both are committed.

Compromise doesn't mean losing yourself.

It means being flexible without breaking your spirit.

And love doesn't mean never hurting each other.

It means repairing gently. It means saying sorry. It means asking, "How can I do better?"

Both partners must show up.

Emotionally. Spiritually. Practically.

It is no longer enough for one person to carry the emotional weight of the entire relationship. That's not love. That's imbalance.

Love isn't perfect.
But when it's conscious – when it's rooted in presence – it becomes the ground where both people can stand tall in their truth.

So don't wait to be whole before you love.
But do make sure you're not looking for someone else to rescue you from your own healing.

Because when two full souls meet – they don't complete each other.

They expand.

Conclusion

This Is for All of Us

This book began with the voice of a woman — but it is for all of us.
For every soul that has stayed too long.
For every person who has loved with more than they had.
For every heart still learning how to receive.

Yes, I wrote through the lens of my own experience — as a woman, as a mother, as someone who has carried the emotional weight of many relationships.
But as I listened, as I spoke to others, I saw something clearly:

Pain has no gender. Patterns have no boundaries.

I met men who were never allowed to cry.
Men who gave everything they had, but still felt unseen.
Men who stayed quiet to keep the peace.
Men who broke down in silence, because the world told them strength meant suppression.

I met women who carried the house, the family, the emotional tone — while smiling through exhaustion.
And others who had shut down completely, tired of being strong all the time.

This is not about who hurts more.
This is not about blame.
This is about understanding where it all comes from — and what we can do with it now.

We all carry patterns.
We all want to be loved.
We all get it wrong sometimes.
We all crave safety, but forget that it must first live inside us.

So let this book not just be a story of grief and healing — but of **returning to balance.**
Let it be a reminder that compromise is not weakness. Adjustment is not defeat.
But putting the burden of healing on one partner — while the other watches from a distance — is not love. That is emotional inequality.

To build something real, we must begin with ourselves.

And then — from that place of self-awareness, fullness, and quiet strength — we meet the other.

Not to complete us.

Not to fix us.

But to walk beside us.

Because only when you are full of love — not from others, but from within — can you truly pour it into someone else without draining yourself.

Whether you are a man or a woman, whether you are healing or holding space, whether you are beginning or ending –

this is for you.

May you always remember:
You were never too much.
You were never not enough.
You are worthy of love that doesn't ask you to disappear.

Let's all become whole in ourselves – and from there, let's learn to love again.

And Finally…

There's still so much I haven't said.

There are still parts of my journey with love – the kind that hurt, the kind that healed, the kind that changed everything – that I've held back.

Not because they don't matter.
But because some stories need more space.
Some truths need more time.
And some healing needs to happen before it can be shared.

Maybe that will become another book.
Another offering.
Another unfolding.

But for now – this is what I had to say.
And I hope it met you, wherever you are, with gentleness and truth.